*The stories in this book are genuine, real, and inspirational. It is not just about dogs and roses. It is also about taking a moment to enjoy and appreciate life. You will learn many beautiful lessons. Some weekends I walk at Balboa Park with Rosalyn and have seen how she connects with people and dog owners with grace and ease. She has the gift to make people comfortable. The way she spots roses and captures their beauty in natural form are real and that's what I like about reading the stories in this book. If you ever need a natural jolt of good feeling, this is a must-read book from a loving and kind author who is passionate about life.*

*"These are lotus seeds from the lotus flowers. They are delicious. If you ever get a chance to visit Cambodia, make sure you have some."*

-Danielle Khim, Executive Coach and Speaker
Email: Danielle@hypnosmot.com
Facebook: www.facebook.com/hypnosmot

*Rosalyn Kahn's book is for dog lovers everywhere and for those who love the beauty of the rose and all of nature. Her book will lift your spirit, make you smile, warm your heart, and touch your soul. You can feel the love that went into every page of this book. A must read for all pet owners and nature lovers everywhere.*

*Denise Carroll, Pet Specialist*

*Rosalyn combined her love of animals, her spirit and deep understand of people in this beautiful book. Get it as a gift to yourself and others of any age. You'll love the precious moments. Hearts around the world have been tapped and the love flows to the beholder!*

*Patty DeDominic*
*Entrepreneurs Coach*

*This is a great book to read for those in the hospital, recovery and rehabs, hospice, child rearing, psychiatric floors, schools, etc.*

*Songwriting Shane*
*Singer/Songwriter/Recording Artist*

*I have been dog sitting for Rosalyn and her husband, David for 11 years. During that time, I have seen them own two dogs, Holly and Scruffy I can truly tell that Rosalyn is a caring and compassionate dog owner. In reading her book, it was fun to see all the cute pictures and great stories. As a dog sitter, it left me with a huge smile. I know you will enjoy reading the book too.*

*Christy Klein, with Christy's Pet Care,*
*818—422-1349 maggieoscar2@comcast.com*

*Rosalyn's powerful book captures your heat, encourages your spirit, and reminds to stop and smell the roses along the path in life while making sure to connect, pet and celebrate the wonderful dogs you meet along the way. It will remind you to pause, be present, enjoy the power of being and connection. Enjoy this beautiful book! :)*

*--Rebecca Hall Gruyter,*
*Founder of Your Purpose Driven Practice and CEO of RHG Media Productions*
*Rebecca@YourPurposeDrivenPractice.com*
*www.YourPurposeDrivenPractice.com   www.RHGTVNetwork.com*

*I met Rosalyn over six months ago and from the moment we met and she shared her ambition for this book Dogs and Roses I was immediately captivated. She couldn't wait to share the draft of her book. Since then I have been following her post on social media about this book and I know it is a winner. This woman has a heart of gold and her love for the dogs and roses is one of a kind. It is a true testament to her heart that she is giving a donation back. In between her call to me she has narrowed down which organization receive the benefits. I have read the book from beginning to end and the picture on the cover is only the beginning you will not want to put this down. You will certain want to tell your friends. Dogs and Roses an inspirational picture and story book certain to change the way you feel.*

*Laurie Lewis Whitney, Humanitarian and Author*

"Not just filled with great photos and quotes, "Dogs & Roses" lends tranquility and deeper understanding about man's, woman's and children's best friends - our dogs. Thank you for including our dog rescues and veterans as beneficiaries of your proceeds."

*Pink Lady Says*

I was honored to receive the book titled "Dogs &Roses" from the incredible writer Rosalyn Kahn, who I admire tremendously for her love of nature and dogs. As a pet parent of a five-year-old pug and an eight-month-old French bulldog, I love the stories and photos. Thank you so much. Keep writing.

*Uleyma Silva, Mrs. Latina Global 2018*

I'm enjoyed the book 100%. This wonderful book stimulating my soul. Remain me, One of the greatest thing in the world. Is the pure and unconditional love of Pets. And the amazing smell of the Nature.
Thank you! Rosalyn Kahn,
With all my appreciation
Alma Dang

Laurie Lewis Whitney's rescue dog

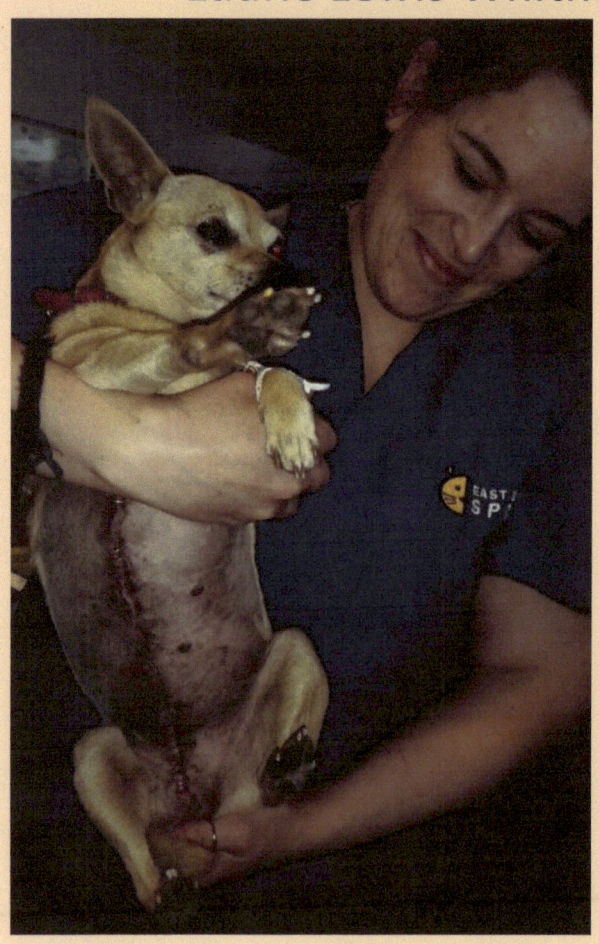

*Meet my childhood hero Heidi*

# Dogs and Roses

## Reducing Stress and Anxiety in Today's Troubled Times

## Rosalyn Kahn

Dogs and Roses

**Dogs and Roses**

By Rosalyn Kahn

© 2017 by Rosalyn Kahn

Published by Solutions Press

ISBN: 978-0-9846872-8-2

All rights reserved. Except as permitted by applicable copyright laws, no part of this book may be reproduced, duplicated, sold or distributed in any form or by any means, either mechanical, by photocopy, electronic, or by computer, or stored in a database or retrieval system, without the express written permission of the publisher, except for brief quotations by reviewers.

# Contents

| | |
|---|---|
| Dedication | v |
| Foreword | vi |
| Foreword | viii |
| Introduction | ix |
| A Walk in the Park | 1 |
| The Little White Dog | 4 |
| Scooby and Tank "Just waiting…." | 6 |
| Alone with the Memories | 7 |
| Both Beautiful in Their Own Way | 8 |
| Today's Adventure | 9 |
| A Special Bouquet | 12 |
| Living with Mother Nature | 13 |
| Met on a weekend walk in my neighborhood | 16 |
| Beautiful Flowers | 17 |
| Vet Finds Comfort Returning Home | 20 |
| Manchitas, the Canine Mexican Immigrant | 23 |
| Sally the Dog, the Healer | 25 |
| Fascinating Dogs! | 27 |
| Two Fun Dogs | 32 |
| Wildflowers of Two Kinds | 33 |
| Foxy the Hound | 36 |
| Out for a Ride… | 38 |
| The Beauty of a Single Rose | 39 |
| Prize Pink! | 41 |
| Out in Style | 42 |
| Rose Tea? What an Idea | 43 |
| The Healing Power of Pets for Elderly People | 44 |
| Why should you have a dog? | 50 |
| Check out these reasons; they will blow your mind | 50 |
| A Riot of Flowers! | 54 |
| The Love of Dogs | 55 |
| Dogs and I are Natural Best Friends | 56 |
| Dangers of Commercial Roses | 57 |
| Ensure a Rose Smells as Sweet | 57 |
| Dew at Daybreak | 58 |

# Dogs and Roses

| | |
|---|---|
| Priceless! | 59 |
| Oso | 60 |
| What Dogs Offer Us | 65 |
| What a Beauty! | 66 |
| Always Ready for a Treat | 67 |
| The Vibrant Beauty of the Lotus | 69 |
| Mod Squad: Pepper, Zoey and Jack | 70 |
| Dogs improve our social skills. | 72 |
| Reaching for Heaven | 73 |
| A Convention of Dogs | 74 |
| Elegance in Nature | 75 |
| New Life for Three Dogs | 76 |
| Doron Gazit's Roses | 78 |
| The Delicate Ballerina | 81 |
| Pitter Patter of his Feet Match my Heartbeat | 82 |
| Hamburger Anyone? | 84 |
| Just Hanging Out in the Ocean and the Garden | 85 |
| Dog Story to Warm Your Heart from Reggie Odom | 86 |
| A "Royal" Costume | 88 |
| Benefits of Dogs: Lower Blood Pressure | 89 |
| Dogs are Therapy, Too | 92 |
| Dogs in their Final Moments | 93 |
| Time for Lunch! | 94 |
| The Endless Enthusiasm of Dogs | 96 |
| Moose | 96 |
| A Dog in Winter! | 98 |
| The Odd Couple | 99 |
| The End of Our Journey | 100 |
| Resources | 101 |
| Biography | 104 |
| In Memory of Holly | 105 |

Dogs and Roses
# Dedication

I dedicate this book to my dog Holly, *a Terrier-Shepherd*, who is growing old and may soon leave this life, and to my two favorite passions, Dogs and Roses, both of which bring calm and serenity to my world.

*My husband David and Holly*

Today, as people rush to their next appointments, they neglect to celebrate the value of the present moment, the only place we can truly live.

When in my silent home, I scramble out of bed between 3 and 5 a.m., my dog smiles back at me. She cuddles next to me as I meditate. She joins me when I sigh. Together, we relax.

I also dedicate this book to the other dogs who have brightened my life: Heidi, a Collie; Clancy, a Cockapoo; Clea, a Wolf-Shepherd; Lucky, a Schnoodle; and Scruffy, a Bichon Frise.

And I dedicate it to the dogs I see passing in the street as I walk or drive by. They all have the same effect. They bring a smile to my face.

Dogs and Roses
# Foreword

by Amy Ballard

Our rescue dog, Pippa, inspired my husband and me to keep going when my husband was near death.

Every year we participate in a 5k walk around the Rose Bowl in Pasadena, CA to raise money for a local animal shelter. My husband, Justin, had committed to participating in the 2015 walk a year prior, in 2014. However, shortly after making that commitment, he became seriously ill. He lost over 100 pounds in one year, needed a wheelchair to travel long distances, and faced a bleak future with little hope of a cure.

However, despite his illness, he was determined to honor his commitment to Pippa and to other animals like her who needed a home. In the weeks leading up to the walk, Pippa consistently lay down next to Justin, leaning up against the exact parts of his legs that hurt him the most and acting as a heating pad for him.

Justin often got sick in the middle of the night and slept on the couch since it was close to the restroom. On these occasions, Pippa spent the entire night traveling back and forth between our bedroom and the couch, checking on both Justin and me. She somehow knew that we were both going through a rough time and that we needed her.

The walk gave us purpose and something to look forward to. We assembled a team and marketed the walk via social media. We even had the honor of promoting the walk in our local newspaper and television newscasts when these outlets featured stories about Justin.

On the day of the walk, our team pushed Justin around the Rose Bowl in a wheelchair while Pippa walked alongside him. Justin fulfilled his goal of participating in the walk despite the tremendous pain he endured even while sitting in his wheelchair. The support we received from our friends, family, and Pippa and our ability to contribute to a worthy cause reminded us of life's beauty and motivated us to keep going.

## Dogs and Roses

Justin vowed that day that he would participate in the 2016 walk without a wheelchair. One year later, after going through a major health journey and implementing holistic remedies, Justin completed the 5k walk on his own two feet with Pippa by his side.

In this book, Rosalyn highlights the numerous physical and mental health benefits of dog ownership, which I have witnessed first-hand via my dog's incredible intuition and therapeutic behavior.

Since there are millions of homeless dogs in the world today, we have a wonderful opportunity to adopt a win-win situation for ourselves and them. We can support each other through life's journey.

Through her words and images, Rosalyn also reminds us to appreciate the beauty of life in each moment while practicing mindfulness and gratitude. Dogs are perhaps our greatest teachers of these concepts, as they perpetually live in the present, loving unconditionally without regrets about the past or worry about the future. Similarly, taking a moment to admire the beauty of roses makes us appreciate the here and now. Amid the constant demands and challenges of today's fast-paced world, Rosalyn's book is a tool and a gift to help us unwind and focus on positivity and beauty.

Dogs and Roses
# Foreword

by Reggie Odom
Spiritual Teacher, Transformational Speaker and Seminar Leader
(*The Ten Commandments of Greatness, The Uncommon Success Seminar & Intimate*)

After reading Rosalyn's book, *Dogs and Roses*, I feel as if I have just been on the most wonderful vacation. I am touched, happy, relaxed, feel uplifted and write with a smile as my spirit is refreshed by the beauty and love in the many colors, sizes, shapes, forms and personalities found within these pages. Roz has created this journey through two of the most wonderful gifts we humans have been given – dogs and roses, not necessarily in that order.

Roz writes and photographs with the Spirit and heart of someone who deeply sees, appreciates and is able to deliver to us the individuality and beauty of each dog; their healing, joy bringing and even life changing qualities; and the unique relationship and bond between dogs and their people.

She not only sees and appreciates the beauty and qualities of the rose itself. She also communicates the transformative qualities of this beauty such that we, the readers, experience it. It's an interesting juxtaposition of dogs and roses through words and photographs. They work like a beautiful whole to light up the soul.

I hope many people, both lovers of dogs and roses, and those who don't generally take time to "stop and smell the roses" or to be touched and lit up by the unaffected, pure spirit of dogs will begin this book. You will be eager for more with each page.

Dogs and Roses

# Introduction

This book is meant to be dipped into and savored any time you need to escape the rush of the outside world and experience the peace and beauty that both dogs and roses give us. Look at it as a random walk in the park, where you can see happy dogs trotting past beautiful roses.

Roses are special to me. My name includes a rose, my garden growing up was filled with roses, my wedding dress had roses embedded in the lace fabric and my anniversary coincides with the annual Pasadena Tournament of Roses Parade.

Dogs are also special to me, as you can see from the dedication. They have always been part of my life and will always be.

Dogs and roses above all offer sanctuary from those hectic, hurried days where stress and agitation impinge on our world. Taking a moment to observe the beauty of roses quiets the storms between my ears and brings me back to peace and calm.

Dogs and roses allow us to escape the structured boxes that often restrict our lives. They don't care when we pay attention to them. They only care that we notice them and allow their loyalty and beauty to inspire us. In this book, you will step away from the world that demands constant attention to a world that allows random interest. Join me on a journey through this neglected world where surprises lurk around every corner (and on every page) and a laugh, a tear, or just a sigh, is never far away. May these photos and statements offer you a moment to step back, unwind, and simply appreciate life's beauty.

# A Walk in the Park

*Dogs and nature share a similar quality. They change with the seasons and they boost your mood to help you feel better. I don't know this little dog but I can tell she loves me.*

*Isn't this just the cutest little pup?*  *Congo*

# Dogs and Roses

*Vanilla, Strawberry, and Chocolate as I walked past them in a West Covina park.*

*This lemon-yellow rose unwraps like a twisting kaleidoscope*

# Dogs and Roses

*Ben and Fred enjoying a beautiful day outside.*

## The Little White Dog...

*Bob shared this story of a white dog that looked pretty much like the one in the photo to the right. Let's slide back 20 years to a time when people could bring their pets on board airplanes with no problem.*

*A passenger reclines in his seat about to doze off when he catches a glimpse of a flash of white pass by his feet. He glances around and sees nothing. A few minutes later he sees the same white flash go the other way.*

*Then the airline stewardess says over the intercom, "Would the owner of the white poodle mix please ring your bell for your dog to return to you."*

*The owner had fallen fast asleep and the young puppy had managed to find his way out.*

*Everyone on the plane laughed.*

# Dogs and Roses

## Scooby and Tank "Just waiting…."

# Alone with the Memories

Appreciate the beauty of this delicate rose today, as tomorrow it will be another memory.

*This lilac rose reminds me of a special memory.*

# Both Beautiful in Their Own Way

*"The weather back home was more tolerable. The humidity here is unbearable."*

*Could Mother Nature have picked a more eloquent design?*

# Today's Adventure

Dogs and Roses

*Hobo and his bottles!*

Dogs and Roses

*Hobo enjoying his favorite toy*

Dogs and Roses
# A Special Bouquet

*The rose and the thorn are a gentle reminder of the victories and perils that make life special.*

Dogs and Roses
# Living with Mother Nature

"A dog is a vehicle, you know; a dog is a window to Mother Nature, and that's the closest species we have." --Cesar Millan

Read more: http://www.brainyquote.com/search_results.html?q=Dog+quote

*Chico: Shy and demure. "I was scolded in the past for making eye contact."*

## Dogs and Roses

*Sunlight adds a startling effect to the glistening center of this.*

*Riley in the tender care of dog sitter Veronica!*

# Dogs and Roses

*Lily Smith: "I really could do without the plaid comforter and a yellow ribbon is not my style. Why not give a dog as a wedding gift?*

# Met on a weekend walk in my neighborhood

# Beautiful Flowers

*Part of a summer project where I made and shared one bouquet every day and created a lot of new friendships.*

# Dogs and Roses

*Beautiful rose from Wendy Lynn Adams*

# Vet Finds Comfort Returning Home

*Luis Rosario's wife, Samantha found this dog, Elsie, about two months after Luis left the military service but Luis didn't want the dog.*

*Luis had been out for about six months when his wife's schedule changed. She had to wake up at four a.m. and leave the house at 5:15 a.m. She didn't return until 7 PM.*

*There was no way that Luis could speak to his wife during the day as she worked with the military with sensitive information. His only buddy was Elsie. In the moments of sadness when he would cry, Elsie would give him kisses. They've been nearly inseparable ever since.*

*His story inspired me to donate the proceeds from this book to help veterans like him.*

*Luis Rosario with Elsie*

# Dogs and Roses

*Handicapped veteran Cari van Sternberg and Puki lives at Olive Branch Retirement Center*

Dogs and Roses

*Charles Arrieta, from a family of veterans, owner of Olive Branch Retirement Center in Reseda, shares his dog Paxo with veterans and senior citizens.*

# Manchitas, the Canine Mexican Immigrant

By Lee Pound

Speaker, Coach, Writing Trainer

Excerpted from *Nine Days in November*, by Lee Pound, to be published in the Fall of 2017. Used with permission of the author.

In the last part of 1997, my wife Sheri mentioned she wanted a dog. I had not had one since elementary school, when we had a cute mongrel named Butch in the back yard. I didn't want a dog since we already had cats but Sheri kept up talk about the wonderful dogs she had as a child so the discussion continued but no action ensued.

As an aside, the dogs she had were the one part of her home life she liked. The memory must have stuck as she had several dogs in her Tucson and Hemet days. The dog in many ways gave her the comfort she needed to feel safe.

The next summer, the family of her godson invited us to return to Mexico because Paco had opened a new veterinary clinic with a friend and he also wanted to show us around the area. We caught a plane and headed south again.

As soon as we arrived, dogs surrounded us. They barked all day and barked all night. At the vet clinic, in one back room we saw a dozen cages, each with a dog inside. Sheri noticed this cute puppy, white with rust-colored markings. The next day she walked the pup with Paco and his other dogs. This curious, active, and healthy if a bit flea-bitten dog captured her heart.

Paco raised show dogs and entered them in local and regional contests. He had several champions and many excellent placers.

One day, Sheri asked where the pup she liked had come from. Paco said they had left the door open a few minutes too long one night before he locked up. When they

## Dogs and Roses

*Sheri, Lee and Manchitas c 2000*

arrived the next morning, they found the pup inside and nobody had the heart to throw her out.

She asked Paco's wife, "What will you do with the dog?"

"She's not a show dog. We will have to give her away."

"No, you won't," Sheri said. "We'll take her home." She turned to me. "Won't we!" I nodded. What else could I do?

Attention turned to how this might be done. It is not easy to transfer dogs from one country to another. We found it might be harder to take the dog out of Mexico than to get her into the United States. We needed a veterinarian to certify she had all her shots and Paco had one on staff. Sheri, as the new owner of the dog, gave her a flea bath (we have photos) and a new name, Manchitas. Manchas in Spanish are spots so the name meant little spots. At the time Manchitas fit into two hands like a tiny ball of fur. We had no idea she would get a lot bigger.

We did the usual visitor stuff for a week or so then prepared to leave. We got the certificate, had the Mexican vet at the airport certify her worthy to depart and got on the plane with Manchitas in a carry box in the passenger cabin.

All went well until we arrived in Dallas, Texas. Well, attempted to arrive. A huge thunderstorm attacked the city and after two passes, the pilot announced we would head to Austin to wait out the storm for two or three hours.

## Dogs and Roses

When we landed in Austin, the government considered the plane to still be in Mexico since we had not yet cleared customs and immigration, which meant nobody got off, including dogs who might need to pee. As we sat in Austin, people on the plane got to know Manchitas. The stewardesses got her water and set out towels in case she needed them.

By the time we headed back to Dallas we had already missed our connecting flight to Orange County and might miss the next one, a nine o'clock flight scheduled to land a few minutes before the Orange County Airport closed.

Of course, the storm had made a mess of air traffic in Dallas. First, we had to get the little dog into the country. The immigration officer asked for her papers, glanced at them and let her pass. We got on the last plane out and waited. Massive numbers of planes waited in line to take off before us.

We got out of the gate, waited, got in line, and after a long wait, took off. The pilot assured us he would work to get us to Orange County on time. You already know what happened next. The plane had to move around big clouds and by the time we got up to speed, the pilot announced we would divert to Los Angeles because Orange County would not stay open for us. They would arrive about midnight, put us on the bus and drive us to Orange County Airport, where would could catch a taxi for home.

We arrived home about 2 a.m., complete with dog we had no idea how to handle, no bed for her, no food for her, no way to control her, and no help in sight.

Manchitas grew up to be a 40-pound bundle of energy, a sweet dog who loved to take long walks and hang out with the cats. She gave us 14 years of pleasure and passed away a few months after we moved to Laguna Woods.

## Sally the Dog, the Healer

In 2014, my wife Sheri got sick. She underwent major surgery in September of that year and was diagnosed with pancreatic cancer. After surgery, she went to a rehab facility a few miles from home to recover. We quickly discovered that the rehab policy

# Dogs and Roses

allowed animals in the rooms, which made rehab bearable. As soon as we discovered this, I began to bring Sally, our little Jack Russell, with me in the evenings.

*Sally with little friend Chico*

Sally got so excited to go to rehab she ran to the car and couldn't wait to get in every night. A hyper little girl, she loved to be included. In the room, she would jump up on the bed and cuddle with Sheri while we watched TV. Sally gave Sheri great comfort and a little bit of home for the months we spent in rehab.

Sheri spent October, November, and early December there, a few miles from home. The staff gave her great care. After a few weeks, they gave her leave to visit the house a few times and for doctor appointments. Sally helped get her through this traumatic period. I'm not sure what we would have done without our loving little pup.

# Fascinating Dogs!

*Maggie, owned by my dog sitter Christy*

Dogs and Roses

"Even show dogs need a disguise." Indiana wearing Shades.

Photo from Steve Carver, artist, instructor in art, photography, and filmmaking

"Man himself cannot express love and humility by external signs so plainly as does a dog, when with dropping ears, hanging lips, flexuous body, and wagging tail, (she) meets (her) beloved master". --Charles Darwin

Hoby

*"It's a long, hot day!"*

Dogs and Roses

*Lucy, the Tibetan Terrier, says "Are we ready yet?"*
*Owner says, "Show me where your leash is."*
*Response? She brings back a stuffed animal and wants to go out the door with it*
*Taken at the Pasadena Rose Bowl.*

## Two Fun Dogs

*Shiva the pit bull and Zive*

Dogs and Roses
# Wildflowers of Two Kinds

*Could it be a sea of wild flowers? No, just my front yard.*

*Owner Lynn Miclea*

# Dogs and Roses

*Peach Powder: Which came first the vine or the flower?*

*Awwwww....Rosie*

*The beauty of this rose is like the pattern of life as we grow from infancy to maturity. According to Rose Magazine, found online, "The rose also offers a soothing property to the nerves and emotional /psychological state of mind. It is regarded as a mild sedative and anti-depressant."*

http://www.rosemagazine.com/

# Foxy the Hound

Terri Fox is the owner of Foxy the Hound.

Terri began her story of how she got started in the animal rescue business. It goes back to the day one of her children brought home a tiny dog the size of her hand. She told her mom the puppy would have to be killed because it was too small and the rescue place did not have a place for small puppies.

Her mom couldn't believe that and the rest is history. She became involved in the animal shelter business, helping many dogs from many places.

Three years have passed since that first dog came home. One of her greatest passions is rescuing dogs on the Fourth of July. Animals undergo enormous shock on this holiday from exploding fireworks. They often run away from their homes and in panic and fear and put their lives at risk. Terri goes out to rescue them. Once back at her place, she checks to see if they have a chip. Then she puts out the word to let people know if they've lost their dog and where they can find it. She used to enjoy the fireworks but now Fourth of July is her biggest rescue day.

I asked if this was typical. She said it was a 365-day job. "I'm always out saving some dog somewhere," she added.

Once she had a request that came in from Oregon. Someone had seen her dogs online and wanted one sent up there to live on a 5-acre plot of land.

If you need a friend in your life to add some joy, call Foxy the Hound.

Dogs and Roses

## Out for a Ride...

*Money can't buy happiness, but the smile of a dog lives in one's heart for eternity.*

*Two dogs near the street at Will Rogers State Beach. A friend told me he had fond memories of his dog as a child. Yet his strongest memory is when he lost his dog due to a car accident. He still carries this painful memory him.*

# The Beauty of a Single Rose

*A single rose in my garden is a wonderful source of comfort.*

# Dogs and Roses

*Daisy the Sheepherder & Buster at Mono Lake*

*What a life! Fresh air and mountain breezes. What else does one need?*

Dogs and Roses
# Prize Pink!

*It is no wonder that I begin each day spraying a soap and water mixture on the roses to protect them against bugs. Little did I know the huge benefit to my mental well-being.*

*Wouldn't you agree this rose is a prime candidate for First Prize at a county fair?*

Dogs and Roses
# Out in Style

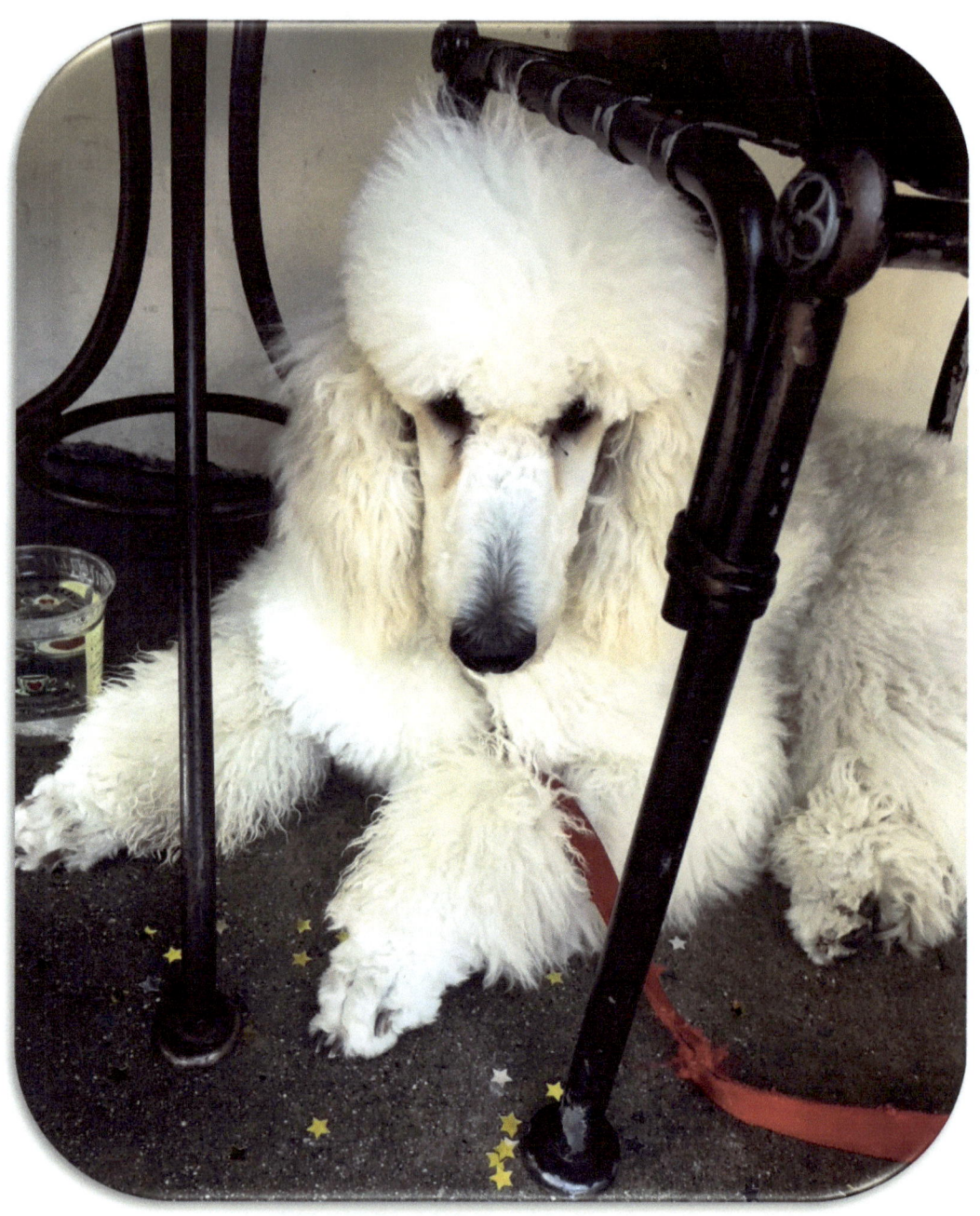

*West Hollywood Style and Fashion*

*"I tell you my boss man says we are going into town for a quick stop and I get stuck here. Give me a break. I just got off the set."*

Dogs and Roses
# Rose Tea? What an Idea

*Triple Crown of Salmon Roses*

*Why not boost your health? Try rose tea.*

*Rose Magazine says: "Rose hips (the flowers which have swollen to seed) are an excellent source of vitamins A, B3, C, D, and E. They also contain bioflavonoids, citric acid, flavonoids, fructose, malic acid, tannins and zinc. Taken in the form of tea, they are good for infections, particularly bladder effects."* http://www.rosemagazine.com/

Dogs and Roses

# The Healing Power of Pets for Elderly People

## Barbara Ballinger, Aging Care.com

For elderly pet owners, who often live alone or in group facilities, pets can help reduce stress, lower blood pressure, increase social interaction and physical activity, and help them learn.

"A new pet can stimulate someone to read up on an animal or breed, which can be very mentally stimulating and important at that age," says Dr. Katharine Hillestad, a veterinarian with the office of Doctors Foster and Smith in Rhinelander, Wisconsin, which provides online advice and retails pet supplies and pharmaceuticals.

Pets provide other intangibles. "Dogs and other pets live very much in the here and now. They don't worry about tomorrow. And tomorrow can be very scary for an older person. By having an animal with that sense of now, it tends to rub off on people," says Dr. Jay P. Granat, a New Jersey psychotherapist.

And pets can reduce depression and lessen loneliness. "Older pet owners have often told us how incredibly barren and lonely their lives were without their pet's companionship, even when there were downsides to owning an active pet," says Linda Anderson, who founded the Angel Animals Network in Minneapolis with her husband Allen. The couple speaks and writes books about the joys of pet ownership.

In *Angel Dogs: Divine Messengers of Love* (New World Library, 2005), the Andersons tell the story of Bonnie, a golden retriever that quickly became an indispensable member of her adoptive family. "We never felt alone when Bonnie was in the house. As we aged and tended to go out less, she provided us with loving companionship," say her owners, Marjorie and Richard Douse.

Psychologist Penny B. Donnenfeld, who brings her golden retriever mix Sandee to her New York City office, has even witnessed animals' ability to rev up elder owners' memories. "I've seen those with memory loss interact and access memories from long ago," she says. "Having a pet helps the senior focus on something other than physical problems and negative preoccupations about loss or aging."

Pets benefit, too, particularly when older folks adopt older pets. "These lucky pets go from the pound to paradise. Since most of the adopters are retired, they have lots of time to devote to a previously unwanted pet," says Chicago veterinarian Tony Kremer, who with his wife Meg operates Help Save Pets—Humane Society, which operates adoption centers.

Here are some things caregivers should consider when purchasing a pet for their senior mom or dad.

Right pet for the right owner. But because people age so differently, the decision needs to be made carefully—and not just by grown, loving children who think it sounds like a way to provide camaraderie. Because there's no single right pet, ask the following questions to help narrow the field, says Dr. Donnenfeld.

Are you set in your ways? If you don't like change, you may not be a good candidate, say the Andersons.

Have you had a pet before? Amy Sherman, a licensed therapist and author of *Distress-Free Aging: A Boomer's Guide to Creating a Fulfilled and Purposeful Life*, thinks it's best if the elderly person is an experienced owner.

Do you have disabilities? Dogs can be wonderful companions who encourage a senior with no major physical limitations to walk and interact with others, Dr. Donnenfeld says. For those who are physically challenged, cats often need less care than dogs, she says. A small dog that's paper-trained or an indoor bird is also sometimes preferable, she says.

Do you need a therapy pet? If the person is very infirm or impaired, they may be a candidate for an assistance or therapy dog to help them function or interact.

Is the pet the right age? A puppy or kitten may not be the best choice for elderly owners because of the care they require. A young pet may outlive its owner. Birds especially have long life spans. Yet, it's also important that the pet isn't too old since it may start to have physical limitations and get sick, Dr. Donnenfeld cautions.

Does the pet have a good temperament? Although some older owners may think a Great Pyrenees would be too big to handle, Daffron found one mixed two-year-old so mellow that it would have been a good pet for a senior. "Many older people might think they'd do better with a Jack Russell terrier because it's small but they are very, very, very high energy and require more effort and commitment. So much depends on personality," she says.

Is the pet healthy? It's important that any pet be examined by a professional. "You don't want to compromise an older person's immune system since some pets carry diseases," says Dr. Hillestad.

One pet or two? While multiple pets can keep each other company, that may not be a good idea for an older person, says Dr. Hillestad. "Two puppies may bond with each other rather than with the owner," she says.

Are finances an issue? Pets cost money. A small puppy can run more than $810 its first year for food, medical care, toys and grooming while a fish is less expensive-- about $235, according to the American Society for the Prevention of Cruelty to Animals. If the pet takes ill, dollars snowball. Groups are available which can help allay costs.

Susan Daffron, author of *Happy Hound: Develop a Great Relationship with Your Adopted Dog or Puppy* (Logical Expressions, 2006), has taken pets to nursing homes through shelter outreach programs. "I go down halls and people will say, 'Oh, this looks just like my dog,'" she says. She has also helped elderly folks adopt the right animal. One woman, 86, wanted to be able to walk a dog but didn't want a hyper pet. "She was good at judging her limitations," Daffron says.

Angie Jones became interested in training therapy dogs after bringing her dog Hunter to visit her late father in a retirement home. "It took us half an hour to get to my dad's room because everyone stopped us along the way and wanted to pet the dog and tell me about their dog," she says. "Hunter brought my father great joy and opened the door of communication since he was more of a recluse," says Jones, who started Central Ohio Good Shepherds, a chapter of Therapy Dogs International Inc.

Where to find the pet. While breeders are a good source, some shelters also provide a pet for less and offer the advantage of rescuing it from euthanasia. Purina Pets for Seniors partners with 200 shelters nationwide to provide seniors pet adoptions at a reduced cost (www.petsforpeople.com). Local services also exist, such as Paws/LA in Los Angeles (www.pawsla.org).

Shelter employees often know the pet's personality well and can make a good match, says Daffron. Online pet shopping is also possible, thanks to sites like www.petfinder.com, which pairs owners with 250,000 adoptable pets from 11,000 animal and rescue groups nationwide.

*"I tell you the ocean breeze beats that rolled-down window."*

How to provide care long-term for a pet. Because an older owner may take ill or die, it's important that the pet is provided for in a will and a caregiver named, says Dr. Hillestad. Even more basic is that someone knows that an elderly person has a pet. "If the person is rushed to the hospital, it could be left alone if nobody knows," says Allen Anderson.

According to a study from SUNY Buffalo (2006), 240 married couples with dogs were subjected to various types of stressful tasks where they were either alone, with their spouse or were able to see their dog before or after the task. Unsurprisingly, the lowest responses to stress were among those who were allowed to see their dogs. Maybe there should be a mandatory "bring your dog to work" day!

The greatest thing in the world is the unconditional and overflowing love a dog gives, often more empowering than one's own self confidence.

# Dogs and Roses

*Dogs can't get any cuter than Lucky!*

*Rose Wreath used at funeral.*
*Rose petal of a heart.*
*Each offers its own beauty.*
*Charlene Capetillo*
*Which path would you choose?*
*Charlene Capetillo*

*Photo taken below Temescal Canyon in Santa Monica*

# Why should you have a dog?
# Check out these reasons; they will blow your mind.

Though my own dog, Holly is not feeling well, she keeps smiling.

Statistics don't tell us everything we need to know, but they can be compelling. According to health organizations, dog owners have:

Lower Cholesterol, Lower blood pressure, and Fewer heart attacks.

In fact, the British Journal of Health (2004) stated that dog owners have fewer medical problems than those without pets!

According to NBC news.com, it can take only about 15 to 20 minutes with a pet to develop calmness and a relaxed attitude.

It may surprise you, but despite my exuberance and light-hearted lifestyle, I still get agitated when things go awry.

I've found that sitting close to my dog, my head next to hers, allows me to become calmer, matching my breath to hers, focusing on the experience. To me, it seems to help us both.

A year later, as she continues to age, my dog, even in her illness, finds comfort sitting in my lap in the early morning or evening when she is restless.

# Dogs and Roses

Dogs and Roses

*Were you looking for me? Here I am.*

# Dogs and Roses

# A Riot of Flowers!

How many pictures could you paint that include the beauty you see below?

*Cornucopia of Roses from Church of Jesus Christ of Latter Day Saints, West Los Angeles*

# The Love of Dogs

Those effects I feel with my dog are not exclusive. They can be transferred to other dogs. Check out these other dogs and the grins on their faces. Sitting and holding a dog brings me eternal peace. No one can love you more than your dog, who senses your every need.

*Lulu and Lucky, DNC Philadelphia. I can tell by hands that hold me there is love between us.*

*Benny, Irvine CA, "I really love the scratch behind my ear. It is perfect."*

# Dogs and I are Natural Best Friends

*Cocoa, Angel in Sherman Oaks*
*"Laying in her arms reminds me of my birth with my mom. What a great dream."*

*Angel, the dog on the right, remembers our meeting six months ago.*

*Cocoa, the dog on the left, had met me five minutes earlier and went to sleep immediately once I began scratching behind his ears.*

*The best friend you'll ever have can be found in a pet store, animal show, or strolling the streets.*

Dogs and Roses

This week I learned about the horrible atrocities caused by the roses produced with the help of pesticides.

# Dangers of Commercial Roses

## Ensure a Rose Smells as Sweet

By Roger Di Silvestro 02-01-2005

Americans will buy about 110 million roses for Valentine's Day gifts. That number and the millions more purchased throughout the year are a boon to the economies of flower-growing nations and, in the short term, for floral workers. But in the long term, those flowers threaten both human and environmental health in those same countries.

Our roses typically come from Ecuador, which is the third largest producer of these products and the net gain for 70 percent of it from roses. The country is the world's fourth-largest producer of roses. Some 60,000 of its citizens work in the business, producing a dozen roses at a cost of about $2. The worker is paid just $125 to $170 monthly.

The roses take 45 – 60 days to grow in tightly constrained greenhouses heavily dependent on pesticides. These often prove deadly to those who care for these roses.

Each rose grower in Ecuador on average uses three poisons to kill worms, four to kill insects, and six for fungi, including several that are tightly restricted in the United States because of their threat to human health. Workers remain in greenhouses while these pesticides are applied. Health ailments among the workers are typical of those resulting from exposure to toxic chemicals, including minor symptoms such as headaches, blurred vision and nausea as well as more severe problems such as still births, birth defects and vaginal bleeding among the women, who make up two-thirds of the floral workforce. In addition, the pesticides poison local water sources and have sickened local livestock.

Consumers can help by purchasing only certified roses.

One solution to the problem would be tighter U.S. restrictions on floral pesticide residues. European nations are already taking such measures to lower the incentive for pesticide use, but the United States is dragging its regulatory heels. Fortunately, consumers also can make a difference. They can purchase greenery—such as ferns, used in virtually all bouquets—that are certified by the nonprofit Rainforest Alliance, which tests standards.

# Dew at Daybreak

*A fresh morning view.*

Dogs and Roses
# Priceless!

*Descanso Gardens- Beauty descends as the chapters of our lives unfold.*

# Oso

*Oso and I met on July 4th as I went down to the ocean to find peace. Oso's eyes see from here to eternity.*

*Denise Carol, a Pet Communicator Specialist, described Oso as, "A healing dog helping people from far and near."*

*No sooner had I arrived than I saw this dog. Its owner was principal of a school where her heart's passion was Random Acts of Kindness, the topic of my last book.*

*The dog can only reflect the view you portray. Dogs have immense power to mimic what they see and what they feel. How many times have I stared into a set of eyes and knew the other side could read fear, just as I did, just like an animal? It also can feel love.*

# Dogs and Roses

*Pure magical magnificence, just like a magician unfurling his cape.*

# Dogs and Roses

# Dogs and Roses

*"Don't give me a hard time. I am having a bad hair day." What are those eyes telling you?*

*Lake Balboa, a favorite place to walk dogs.*

# What Dogs Offer Us

*We spend a lot of time training our dogs. They offer us a lot in return: patience, responsibility and commitment. We gain by thinking less about ourselves and more about others. Pets can be a be a barometer of the good and bad be it a guide dog, airport security, or a military combat dog. Dogs also help people with diseases.*

# What a Beauty!

*Descanso Gardens*

# Always Ready for a Treat

*Imagine waking up each day to see Lulu smiling at you. "The last time I gave a big smile I got a treat. Is this smile big enough?" Temecula Canyon*

# The Vibrant Beauty of the Lotus

*A special story of the lotus flower. A friend of mine had traveled abroad and found one of these gorgeous flowers she wanted to buy. She began conversing with the salesperson and asked how much she earned each day.*

*The person responded in a soft voice, "About $5.00 a day." This is the same price as the cost for food in that area. My friend thought about her life back home and decided to buy a bunch of flowers to help her have a better day.*

*Maybe you will remember this story the next time you travel. --Danielle Khim*

## Mod Squad: Pepper, Zoey and Jack.

Life is like a dogsled team. One never knows where the leader may go. We simply follow for the best adventure.

*"If you can, please tell me where the water hole is located. My buddy in the back needs a restroom and he is a bit shy."*

# Dogs and Roses

*Double the benefits: Improve both your heart and mood with chocolate from Universal City.*

## Dogs improve our social skills.

*"Where is my share of the pancakes? In my house, I have my own place setting. What is wrong with this place?"*

# Reaching for Heaven

*Just as theatre lights shine brightest on the Star, the sun shines brightest on the rose.*

# A Convention of Dogs

[A study by Britain's Warwick University](#) found that 40% of people reported making friends much easier as a result of owning a dog.

Which one of these would you like to walk around with in your neighborhood?

*Can you imagine the fun we had taking this shot? We finally decided to go with the one where the majority of the dogs had smiles.*

Dogs and Roses
# Elegance in Nature

*One royal flush of elegance.*

Dogs and Roses
# New Life for Three Dogs

This next part will break your heart. It comes from my AT&T cell phone agent, Christina in Oklahoma, who heard about my book and decided to send these photos and the following stories.

Tolkke (brown) has had the hardest start to his life and has had the fortune to escape death multiple times. Tolkke was initially a bait dog in a dog fighting ring who was rescued by a local shelter. Due to his untrusting nature towards

most humans, he was not adopted. He was about to be euthanized when a woman with a huge heart and small pocket took him to try and help rehabilitate him. Two weeks after rescuing him, her husband admitted to having a girlfriend for 16 years out of their 25-year marriage. Heartbroken and without a home, she was forced to get rid of Tolkke. He was 30 minutes away from being euthanized when I met him and my heart melted. He

## Dogs and Roses

slowly approached me with his head and body low to the ground. I said, "Come here lil baby" and got down on his level. He immediately ran and jumped on me giving a true hug! I'd never had a dog pull in on a hug and could feel the need for love. My heart instantly melted and I knew Tolkke was mine forever! He is my little shadow. Absolutely! Swizgard is the blonde. We rescued him from a girl who knew her neighbors were running a puppy mill and never reported them. She didn't even like dogs but they were about to take him to be in dog fights, so she took him in for two days. A friend of my husband, Nick, let us know about the dog. We went that very day we were told and saved him from a life of hardships. The black dog (in the same pic) is Roxxo! My cousin found him last August and was going to keep him but their landlord said he looked like a pit bull and he would kick them out if they kept him. My cousin contacted me to see if we would take him in. Since we already had three dogs, we had to see how the others reacted to him. The poor baby was skin and bones! So much to the point that we feared picking him up. The other dogs knew he had suffered much during his short life and immediately accepted him into the Cooper pack! He quickly took to sleeping in the middle and being Swizgard's favorite playmate.

Last but not least is Buddy (older black dog)! He is the oldest and leader, keeping the younger dogs in check if they get too rowdy. He is the best snuggle buddy and has the most expressive eyebrows! The emotion he displays in our day to day activities is above any other animal I have met.

--Christina

# Doron Gazit's Roses

Dorin Gazit: "The Red Line Project is a series of installations in locations around the world devastated by climate change and man's misuse of the environment. So far, I've taken the Red Line to the melting glaciers in Alaska, dry lakes and burnt forests in California and the Dead Sea sinkholes in Israel."

Dogs and Roses

## Meet General after a hard day's work in Brigantine, New Jersey.

*He wants to know why you can't just let sleeping dogs lie and get their rest.*

*He will climb under, jump over and run at the sight of any open door. Yet, by your side, he is the best of friends. He shares the residence with General in Brigatine, NJ.*

This is the same guy sprawled out and sitting straight up. "I know you truly love me!" he says.

This teaches us a lot about gratitude. What else can you learn from your friend?

# The Delicate Ballerina

I see a rose as delicate as a ballerina. The petals shine and spread their wings like a ballerina extends her arms. Yet to earn this place, it is joined by the thorns below to gain support like the hours and blisters the ballerina acquires to reach her prime. A single rose can be more than enough.

*These yellow blossoms remind me of the planets orbiting in our solar system.*

"When autumn darkness falls, we remember the small acts of kindness: a cake, a hug, an invitation to talk, and every single rose. These are all expressions of a nation coming together and caring about its people." --Jens Stoltenberg

Read more at:

http://www.brainyquote.com/search_results.html?q=Rose+quotes+&pg=4

# Pitter Patter of his Feet
# Match my Heartbeat

*"I tell you I don't know what they are going to put on me next...Will you just hurry up with the picture." Compliments of Nadia.*

## Dogs and Roses

*Can you see the way the pink colors of the rose blend in with the peach? This reminds me of a wave breaking on the shore and then rushing back out to sea. These patterns mirror life's changes, going from one year to the next, following life's ups and downs.*

*"This isn't bad for a rest stop but I can't wait until I get home to my own pad."*

We met at a rest stop and he didn't even mind my lame toss. He chased it anyway on the way back from Mono Lake near Independence, California. Then he declared siesta time.

## Hamburger Anyone?

*"They wanted to apply to be in the Guinness Book of World Records to see how many burgers a dog can eat. I already filled up on steaks so I wasn't hungry the time this came out. How else do you think they got the photograph?"*

Dogs and Roses

# Just Hanging Out
# in the Ocean and the Garden

*Brigantine, NJ "Who says a dog doesn't like a cool bath in the ocean. We get hot too!"*

*I find nothing more incredible than capturing the moisture as it clings to its owner's shell.*

Dogs and Roses
# Dog Story to Warm Your Heart
### from Reggie Odom

Sugar is a black Chihuahua with very large ears. One day Obama had a day of Public Service and Reggie decided to go visit the dogs at a nearby Best Friends Animal Society. Her beloved whippet Ollie had passed a little over a year before. She wanted another dog but had mixed emotions, not knowing if she was ready. This was a good foray into the world of dogs.

She visited every one of the dozens of dogs there and was relieved upon leaving that she wasn't compelled to go home with one of them.

As Reggie was leaving the area, a volunteer walked out with a tiny little black dog snuggling in to her shoulder. Like a magnet, Reggie was drawn toward the dog on the woman's shoulder. She learned that this little creature had been a stray for some time and had been badly injured by some large dogs. When someone from the neighborhood brought her into Best Friends in a bloody towel, the doctors weren't sure she would survive. The little dog had been shaking from Day 1.

Reggie asked if she could hold her. She did while she was learning more about the little dog. The conversation turned to Reggie doing partial foster medical care for her. But that was not policy in the organization so they all needed to go talk to the director. While waiting for him to come out, the dog stopped shaking. Reggie said, "Do you see this? She stopped shaking." The volunteer looked knowingly at Reggie and asked, "What do you think that means?" Reggie didn't answer.

*Reggie Odom's dog Sugar*

Partial foster care was a go. Reggie had her for parts of most days, and a couple of overnights. This little dog child healed beautifully and soon was ready for adoption. Reggie said there was no way she was going back to Best Friends to be put up for adoption. Of course, Reggie adopted her and soon named her Sugar as she was so sweet. Reggie beams when she talks about Sugar, who was her first rescue after having dogs for most of her life. She said she wasn't sure who rescued who.

Reggie showed me one video where she had rubbed a special lotion on Sugar's coat intended to soothe her skin. Sugar certainly had other ideas as he scratched, rolled, rooted, tossed, jumped and ran around. It is three years later and the two are inseparable, bringing sweet joy and lightness to each other's world.

Dogs and Roses

*Another cute dog on a walk.*

## A "Royal" Costume

*Riley Herschel Smith. "The kids wanted to dress me up for Halloween and I was part of the Royal Family—Prince Charles"*

# Benefits of Dogs: Lower Blood Pressure

If you look at the number of people who are dog owners, you realize this is no longer just child's play. It seems like everyone has a pet as part of their world. Many people will find a smile on the faces of all who own them. I have several dear friends who love their pets so much they carry them around every day.

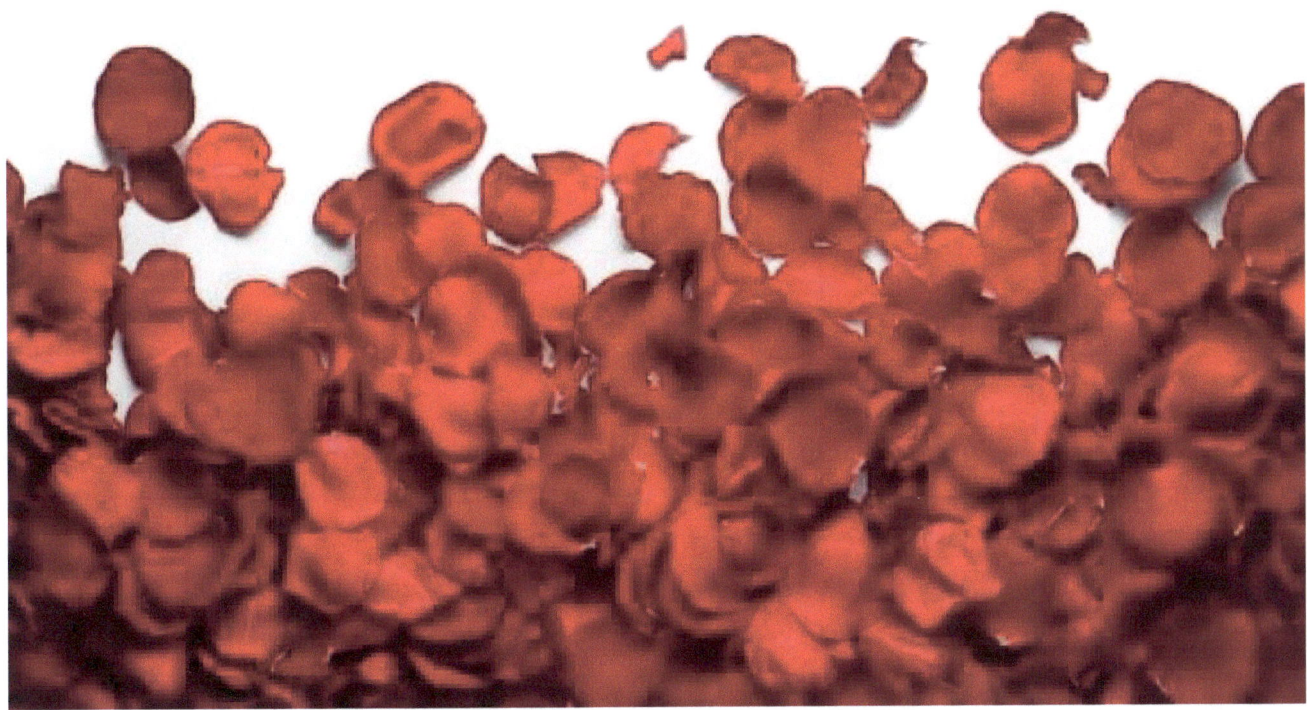

Compliments of Gizomodo.

Currently there are dogs that go to the airport to calm down passengers.

Pets Unstressing Passengers is part of Los Angeles International Airport.

I spoke to the founder, Heidi Huebner, who shared the following via a phone conversation.

It used to be that just three airports had dogs to help passengers. The program has now grown to over 43 airports in Canada, and India. Russia is looking add them as well.

Pets Unstressing Passengers is run entirely by volunteers.

It was founded by Heidi, who had a history in the non-profit world. She formerly owned a targeted non-profit for pets. Then she was promoted to overseeing six animal shelters throughout Los Angeles. Her journey began over six years ago, at LAX. For the first couple of years she did volunteer

# Dogs and Roses

programs. Then three and one-half years ago, at San Jose and Miami, they did the program and realized they could do it in Los Angeles as well. She regularly addressed conferences for 80 other airports and is now a world expert.

Heidi Huebner started a program that helps people reduce the stress and anxiety surrounding today's airport lines and security alerts. All the dogs are registered as therapy dogs with a certificate. Dogs come in all breeds and they can be identified by the red vest they wear around the airport. For more information visit http://www.lawa.org/welcome_LAX.aspx?id=7478

*Dogs of Resistance*

Dogs and Roses

*Cosmo, owned by Jaime and Adrianne Diaz*

# Dogs are Therapy, Too

*"We met by accident but he said we could still be friends."*

Did you know there are therapy dogs for hospice centers? They say that having a dog around may remind them of the comfort they remember having and the dog can sense more acutely where the patient is at the end of their life. All this and more can be found at Therapy Dog International.

Dogs and Roses

# Dogs in their Final Moments

Many people are so attached to their dogs as they enter the last days that instead of seeing people they recall the dogs. Marie described her father Frank Captain, who would see pictures flashing through his mind of his dogs who passed before him. First there was Penny, Misty and then came Molly.

I recall reading a story in a newspaper about a serviceman fighting in the war with his companion dog there to guide him. Typical practice is when the serviceman goes home they may never see their dogs again. One special airline stewardess made it her mission to reunite these two people.

There is even a page on the internet where you can you see great YouTube videos of servicemen being reunited with their dogs.

https://www.buzzfeed.com/chelseamarshall/tear-jerking-moments-of-soldiers-reuniting-with-their-dog?utm_term=.yovmregV3#.odn1Q7pjw

# Time for Lunch!

*The restaurant called to say lunch was ready. My boss said, "Let me grab my dog and we will be on the way." The dog replied, "I am ready and willing to go wherever you go."*

Children learn to read to dogs as therapy to help them read with no judgement. Tail wagging tutors.

Therapy Dog International is an organization founded to help students with low self-esteem issues learn the art of reading. Many find when reading to dogs that it isn't as frightening. Once they sit down and pet the dog, reading becomes much more enjoyable and fun.

# Dogs and Roses

# The Endless Enthusiasm of Dogs

*"I heard part of the proceeds were going to help cute dogs like me. Would you like to donate to help me out?"*

Gratitude beyond Words.

Dogs have endless enthusiasm but never any regrets. I should hire my dog to guide my life.

*Prince Dudeman, all through my dog's eyes*

Dogs and Roses
# Moose

*Moose is enjoying the roses. He heard about the book and decided to pose for this photo.*

# A Dog in Winter!

*Blue, the winter dog, in Eagle, Colorado*

Dogs and Roses
# The Odd Couple

# The End of Our Journey

*It is with a sad goodbye that I come to the close of our journey. I promise there are thousands more photos of adorable dogs, puppies and the most incredible amazing roses where these come from. I promise each is more spectacular than the one before.*

*My dearest hope is that in looking at these photos for just a few moments your heart may open a bit wider to see there is beauty in this world if we allow ourselves to see it.*

Dogs and Roses

# Resources

Wildlife Foundation
Alba Farms, Hollister Salinas
Best Friends
([www.petsforpeople.com](www.petsforpeople.com)).
Local services also exist such as Paws/LA in Los Angeles ([www.pawsla.org](www.pawsla.org)).

**Adoption First Animal Rescue** is a 501 (c)(3) non profit organization recognized by the Internal Revenue Service. Our goal is to rescue dogs of all breeds from county shelters where they could be euthanized.
Founder Staci Ventura and her husband Eric Crespo began to develop the idea of Adoption First Animal Rescue in 2011 while working for a rescue in the San Diego, CA area. When Eric was stationed in North Carolina the two realized how much help the rural areas needed. The two decided to pursue the idea of Adoption First! The Rescue officially started on October 1, 2013 and received its 501c3 status as an official non profit organization in 2014. Since then the rescue has developed a great team of volunteers and have established a board of directors.
North Carolina
http://www.adoption-first.org/ located in North Carolina
PO BOX 1500 Richlands NC 28574

http://www.acepetresort.com/dogs-2/ Pet Resort in Sarasota, Florida
7950 S.R. 72 (Clark Road), Sarasota
Mon. to Sun. 8 a.m. - 1 p.m.
& 3 p.m. - 5:30 p.m.
CLOSED between 1 p.m. - 3 p.m.

**ACE Pet Resort**
They also offers a separate organization Vintage Paws for Dogs older than 10
It rescues them and provides medicine care
vintagepaws.org
Bradenton
941.708.0811
5016 E SR 64, Bradenton
Mon. to Sat. 7 a.m. - 1 p.m.
& 3 p.m. - 6 p.m.
Sun. 9 a.m. - 2 p.m.
CLOSED between 1 p.m. - 3 p.m.

# Dogs and Roses

### Sacred Heart Dog House Doggie Day Care and Boarding
5213 E. Conant Street
Long Beach, CA 90808
562 265 -2913
Veronicadurre@gmail.com
sacredheartdoghouse on instragram

### Barking Hound Village
Pet boarding service in Atlanta, Georgia
Address: 1918 Cheshire Bridge Rd NE, Atlanta, GA 30324
Hours: Open today · 7:30AM–8PM
Phone: (404) 897-3422
Author's note: in my effort to help those in need who require service dogs, I have included some links to help you better understand the problem. Please recognize the laws may vary dependent on the state and county you live in.

### VCA Adler Animal Hospital and Pet Resort
16911 Roscoe Blvd.
North Hills, CA 91343
Tel: 818-893-6366
Fax: 818-894-4310
Monday-Friday:
7:00 am - 8:00 pm
Saturday-Sunday:
8:00 am - 5:00 pm

### Resource for service dogs:
https://www.ada.gov/service_animals_2010.htm
Unraveling the current controversy of service dogs vs. emotional support.
https://www.petfinder.com/animal-shelters-and-rescues/volunteering-with-dogs/service-dog-vs-therapy-dogs/
http://www.petful.com/service-animal/fake-service-dogs/

## Everything you want to Know about Roses and More

### Rose Care

### Rose Resources
http://www.rosemagazine.com/

### How to Start a Rose Garden
https://www.gardeningknowhow.com/ornamental/flowers/roses/starting-a-rose-garden.htm

### Treating your roses
www.almanac.com/plant/roses

### Sun or Shade
http://www.bhg.com/gardening/flowers/roses/rose-care-qa/

### Best Places to View Roses
https://www.latourist.com/index.php?page=rose-parade-tips

### Mental Benefits of Roses
https://www.saga.co.uk/magazine/health-wellbeing/mind/how-smell-affects-your-body-and-mind.aspx

### Benefits of Rose Oil
https://www.organicfacts.net/health-benefits/essential-oils/health-benefits-of-rose-essential-oil.html

### Magic and Mystery of Love Potion
http://everydayroots.com/love-potion

# Biography

Rosalyn Kahn is an author, college professor, professional speaker and Executive Coach. Her first book was *Random Acts of Kindness are Changing the World*. Rosalyn has spoken internationally, having given a book signing for her last book in Rome, Italy. She has done several hundred speeches and delivered three TEDx talks to youth, *Language Come to Life* at Tedx Conejo, *Coming Around the Curve* at Tedx South Hills High, and *Breaking Cultural Barriers* at Tedx Walnut. All can be viewed on her webpage at www.rosalynkahn.com

The inspiration for this book came through her life coach where she began to look inside on what truly brought her joy and happiness. Rosalyn is an avid fan of nature. Her husband bought her as a first anniversary gift a lifetime membership to the Sierra slub. It is in these outdoor trips she was always fascinated by the roses along the way and dogs on her path. "It seemed they were calling out to me," she says. Her husband is just as dedicated to his love of dogs as well.

"As an individual with a huge heart," Rosalyn says, "I asked myself if I could find a gift to share with humanity that would heal the soul. This is the book. My deepest goal is that you flip through these pages from wherever you begin. May you reach the end with a smile in your soul."

Gratitude Beyond Words

From my heart to yours a great big hug

# In Memory of Holly

www.ingramcontent.com/pod-product-compliance
Lightning Source LLC
Chambersburg PA
CBHW042022150426
43198CB00002B/38